4/16

DISCARD

AMAZING INVENTIONS

TELEPHONE

MARY ELIZABETH SALZMANN

Consulting Editor, Diane Craig, M.A./Reading Specialist

Sandcastle

An Imprint of Abdo Publishing
abdopublishing.com

abdopublishing.com

Published by Abdo Publishing, a division of ABDO, PO Box 398166, Minneapolis, Minnesota 55439. Copyright © 2016 by Abdo Consulting Group, Inc. International copyrights reserved in all countries. No part of this book may be reproduced in any form without written permission from the publisher. SandCastle™ is a trademark and logo of Abdo Publishing.

Printed in the United States of America, North Mankato, Minnesota

062015
092015

Editor: Alex Kuskowski
Content Developer: Nancy Tuminelly
Cover and Interior Design and Production: Mighty Media, Inc.
Photo Credits: Library of Congress, Shutterstock

Library of Congress Cataloging-in-Publication Data

Salzmann, Mary Elizabeth, 1968- author.
  Telephone / Mary Elizabeth Salzmann ; consulting editor, Diane Craig, M.A./Reading Specialist.
    pages cm. -- (Amazing inventions)
  Audience: Grades PreK-3.
  ISBN 978-1-62403-712-2
  1. Telephone--Juvenile literature. 2. Inventions--History--Juvenile literature. I. Title.
  TK6165.S25 2016
  621.385--dc23
              2014045329

SandCastle™ Level: Transitional

SandCastle™ books are created by a team of professional educators, reading specialists, and content developers around five essential components—phonemic awareness, phonics, vocabulary, text comprehension, and fluency—to assist young readers as they develop reading skills and strategies and increase their general knowledge. All books are written, reviewed, and leveled for guided reading, early reading intervention, and Accelerated Reader™ programs for use in shared, guided, and independent reading and writing activities to support a balanced approach to literacy instruction. The SandCastle™ series has four levels that correspond to early literacy development. The levels are provided to help teachers and parents select appropriate books for young readers.

EMERGING · BEGINNING · TRANSITIONAL · FLUENT

CONTENTS

ALL ABOUT TELEPHONES

The telephone was invented in 1876.
The first ones didn't have numbers.

You had to talk to an **operator**.
You told the operator whom to call.

Dial phones came out in the 1890s.
People didn't need **operators**.

AT&T invented phones with buttons in 1963.

Many phones send sounds over wires.

They are **landline** phones.

Mobile phones don't use wires.
They send sounds through the air.

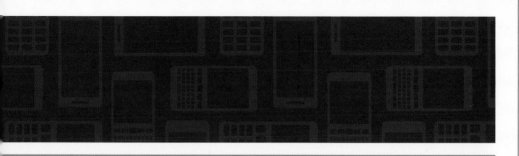

Telephones let people talk to each other.

Carrie calls her grandma.

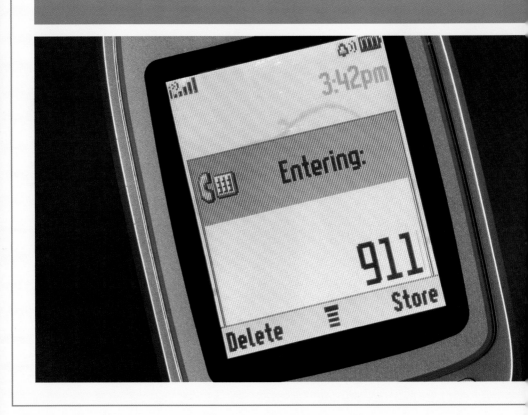

Telephones let people call for help.

Max **dials** 9-1-1.

Smartphones are small computers.

They have cameras, games, and more!

THINK ABOUT IT

Count the phones in your house.
What kinds are they?

GLOSSARY

dial – 1. the part of a telephone that has numbers. 2. to enter a phone number on a telephone.

landline – a telephone that is connected to other telephones through a cable or wire.

mobile – able to be easily carried or moved.

operator – someone whose job is to connect telephone calls.